MY DAY

WHEN YOUR LIFE BECOMES A UNFORESEEN BATTLEFIELD

What Do You Do?

Dr. Monica Johnson

IBG Publications, LLC

Published by I.B.G. Publications, LLC, a Power to Wealth Company

Web Address: WWW.IBGPublications.Com
admin@IBGPublications.Com / 904-419-9810

IBG Publications, LLC, New Castle, Pennsylvania 16101

Johnson, Monica
MY DAY: When Your Life Becomes An Unforeseen Battlefield, What Do You Do?

Printed in the United States of America.

Dedication

This book is dedicated to anyone who has found themselves in an unfamiliar place.

Unfamiliar with feeling as though life has dealt a hand of uncertainties, mind racing thoughts and needing encouragement without judgment.

Just as a butterfly has different seasons, so do you. Always know that your unforeseen battlefield seasons have a time limit with an outcome that is determined by your willingness to transform from **MAYDAY** to **MY DAY** with the use of daily Affirmations!

TABLE OF CONTENTS

Acknowledgments

This book is based on 27 years of encouraging and affirming many and has resulted in a compilation of quotes.

Even though these are some of the quotes I may use daily, I didn't find the time to collectively put them in one place until the pandemic. During the pandemic, my Husband became ill with covid-19. If anyone has ever had a loved one that was ill and you were the spouse, care giver, cook, cleaner, prayer warrior and still had to work, then you can understand the mounting amount of stress that comes along with it.

As ironic as it sounds during that time, I was able to find journaling quotes as a coping mechanism. During my husband's 10-day illness my body was physically tired but, my mind was rejuvenated daily. It was amazing how 27 years of being in the health care field helped me mentally get through a time that was very overwhelming.

I would like to thank my publisher Audrea V. Heard with IBG for being a great support and a true jewel throughout this process.

I would like to thank every patient/client/individual that I've had the opportunity to encourage, educate and motivate during their times of despair with hope, reassurance and mindful transformations.

I would like to thank every co-worker that I've had the opportunity to work beside and every organization that I've worked for that provided me the platform to have an opportunity to make positive changes within the community.

I would like to thank my spiritual parents Bishop Lewis Williams & Dr. Bernadette Williams for their continual prayers and guidance since January 2000.

I would like to thank my parents: Gregory Fields Sr, Mary Fields and my siblings for their love and support in all that I do.

Finally, I would like to acknowledge with gratitude, the support and unwavering love of my Husband and children. I would like to thank my husband: Ervin Johnson Sr., our daughter Emiyah Johnson and our son Ervin Johnson, Jr.

You three give me so much life. Although I have degrees and accolades, you all are my greatest accomplishments. Others have seen me at my best but, you all have seen me when I've given so much of myself to others and had nothing left.

Your unconditional love gives me the fuel that I need to never allow my desire for helping others to diminish.

Without you all, a great deal of what I do or have accomplished would not be possible. Thank you for allowing me to be me.

MAYDAY!

MAYDAY!

MAYDAY!

When your life becomes an unforeseen battlefield, what do you do?

Turn **MAYDAY** into **MY DAY** with words of encouragement.

Introduction

Hello, my name is Dr. My Day. I want to welcome you on a journey that will help guide you through the different processes of when the unforeseen battlefields of life happen.

I am sure you have noticed that butterflies have greeted you from the cover of this book. This is because I desire for you to see the beauty your life will become when these quotes help to transform you from the inside out. The goal for you is to turn Mayday into My Day by learning how to effectively identify triggers and learn coping skills to do away with stressful events that cause increased stress, anxiety, depression and even low self-esteem to become the best you that you can be.

I have written these life defining words of encouragement in order to help you along the ever-transforming moments of life. During many times of encouraging others, I've found that words of affirmation can help produce a pathway of successful life changing outcomes. Throughout life, there are times when changes can be traumatic or triumphed. The truth is that many times in life, we face battles. These battles can be due to health, finances, family, work or just life itself.

Your transformation comparison will be to that of a butterfly. A butterfly? You may ask. Yes, a butterfly. Just as you have stages in your life so does a butterfly. The butterfly goes through 4 life cycle stages:

- Egg
- Caterpillar "the feeding stage"
- Pupa "The transition Stage"
- Adult: The reproductive Stage"

For you, the life cycle stages are:

- Egg "the beginning of your conception."
- Caterpillar "The things in life that allowed you to grow or the times in life that you fed on the wrong things that stunted your growth.
- Pupa "Transitioning through different trials tribulations, lessons, disappointments." This is your cocoon stage when the changes of life that are needed to occur internally are not seen externally. The outside isn't appealing but, it's needed to appreciate the internal process of change.

- Adult "reproductive phases of life that produce good or bad outcomes with the opportunities for change or enhancement with the mindset of finishing what's been started without wavering. This is the phase that allows the internal changes to be exhibited externally when you've chosen to turn "MAYDAY" into "My Day" by using the tools learned during the times of your unforeseen battlefield of life.

As you take this journey of new thought supported by encouragement that I present to you, take notes and journal along the way. Reflect on these affirmations of your transformation during times of an unforeseen battlefield.

Remember to Live, Be & StayWell.

Dr. My Day

The green butterfly is a symbol of good. It also represents love. A green butterfly represents prosperity and fair attainments.

The yellow butterfly symbolizes hope and guidance.

Blue butterflies are used not only for their beauty but also to convey the emotions of beauty, joy and hope.

Seeing a white butterfly could be a response to your prayers. The Bible reminds us that God has plans for all of us: "For I know the plans I have for you, declares the Lord, plans for welfare and not for evil, to give you a future and a hope." *(Jeremiah 29:11 ESV)*

Bridging

Your Gaps

While "BRIDGING YOUR LIFE TOGETHER 2 LIVWELL," you must have the determination to *Be Well* by living a lifestyle to *Stay Well*. You do this by speaking daily words of encouragement that will cause connection and reconciliation of positive thoughts to provide the pathways of purposeful living!

"Procrastination keeps you where you are. Becoming Goal Minded takes you where you want to be."

"Life's best medicine is to Accept & Acknowledge it happened while learning how to Let it Go in Order to Grow."

"Being perfect is overrated but, being Your Best is an even playing field for endless possibilities."

"My life, my choice, I choose to live. **Unapologetically!***"*

"Your healing process begins when you realize who you were, who you are, and who you are destined to become."

"Life is like a deck of cards. You will never know what you will be dealt, but your hand will win if your mind can see past your circumstances."

"Your past has come and gone, but your decisions and choices of today will determine your awaiting future."

"Challenges in your life are the building blocks that lead to the implementation of your character and personal triumphs."

"Your brokenness is not to hinder you, but to give you the opportunity to be put back together without seeing your life through the same shattered past."

"Awakening the mind is pertinent to having good health that will promote strength and reduce stress."

Time of Reflection

Take some time to reflect on your goals and life aspirations that you previously procrastinated on. What will you do differently to move forward? How are you choosing to *live*?

Changes of today

for better

tomorrows

"Turning off negativity allows positivity to be consistent and effortlessly done."

"Being effective today will prevent losing everything tomorrow."

"Standing tall together helps to build a strong community. But sitting down individually prevents it from being built."

"Stop living your life trying to prove others wrong. But instead, live your life to prove yourself right."

"You are not your past, so, why are you walking in it? It is time to start living in the here and now to recognize your future is waiting on you."

"What they said has hurt you, but what are you saying that will help you?"

"Having the right mindset allows you to stay ready. With the right mindset, you will not miss the windows of presented opportunities to go and accomplish everything you set your mind to do."

"You gravitated to what you saw in them. Now you are seeing with corrective vision which allows you to remain with them that have no vision."

"If you are plugged in and feel unempowered, there is a strong chance that the power source has a poor connection."

"Identifying challenges and opportunities that can prohibit or promote change by choice is pertinent for not only longevity but, prosperity."

Time of Reflection

Take some time to reflect on ways you can turn off negativity in your life to turn on your positive thoughts.

How does a changed mindset look?

Encouragement

To

Survival

"You may be broken and wounded but, you are here and surviving."

"Knowing that you are worth being found will allow you to no longer feel lost within your community, family, and within yourself."

"Forgiving people and situations are the key essentials for the perfect recipe for healing, health, and prosperity."

"You must stop living in your past in order to begin to live in your future. If you cannot get beyond your past, your future will never be embraced with the purpose to live."

"Key essentials in life are important. They are important because they unlock doors that have allowed depression, anxiety, suicidal thoughts, unforgiveness, harm, hurt and danger to become a revolving reoccurrence that enters and exit our lives. The effects are regrets and limitations intended to become generational curses."

"As life changes so must you. If you do not evolve with life, you will remain the same."

"You must realize that being different is not a disgrace nor a mistake. Instead, it is a testament that you have been wonderfully and beautifully made with the title of being a masterpiece of humanity, a one-of-a-kind earthly treasure."

"Everyone is not your assignment. When you realize this, then and only then will you understand you cannot fix everything and everyone. You will no longer become stressed, which triggers feelings of disappointment."

"Wanting and having only becomes a dilemma when what you have has no purpose and your purpose no longer outweighs what you want."

"Your divine purpose has been held up long enough by you and others. Walking in your purpose on purpose starts by moving out of your own way and taking the restrictions off yourself that you have allowed yourself and others to implement."

Time of Reflection

Here is where you can reflect on times you have gone through challenging times throughout life.

As you stand on this side of victory, what advice would you give your former self, or someone going through a similar battle?

Wisdom

To

Live By

"You do not have what you need because what you want is screaming louder, causing your sense of necessity to become misconstrued and deafening."

"What you say should be meaningful to prevent what you are saying to become meaningless."

"Stress should not be an option, but it is a choice resulting in stressful outcomes. Choose wisely to stress less and not allow stress to be an option."

"Be careful that what or who you are complaining about today does not become who and what someone else will compliment and appreciate tomorrow."

"Encouraging and uplifting others will cost you nothing; but refusing to encourage and uplift others may cost someone who is mentally, emotionally, physically, and spiritually broken everything!"

"It was Delayed in receiving due to procrastination, but it was obtained on time due to proclamation and reciprocity."

"Being married means it is ok to
continue to make each other's day
by doing simple things that
mean so much."

Being married does not mean you
stop dating."

"If you do not make plans for success your plans for failure have already been accomplished."

"Remain vigilant and not fearful; stand firm be strong and fight on!"

"What you thought was sent to destroy you was only a test preparing you for the next season of growth, blessings and maturity."

Time of

Reflection

As you have taken in these words of wisdom, reflect on times when you allowed stress to overtake you.

As you look back now, what would you have done differently to handle the levels of stress you endured?

The

Absolutes Of

Life

"Forgiveness is the pre-requisite that establishes the foundation for the overflow of what God has in store for you and your generations."

"Taking the high road when others went low. While Remaining professional and Poised. Well done."

"Life lessons promote growth only through positive behavior."

"Inspired by true events not deterred by false circumstances."

"Knowing who you were helped you to recognize who you are and realize who you are to become."

"Unapologetically live life because
life will not apologize for you
not living it."

"Never allow your best qualities to
become your worst characteristics."

"Stop looking for free. Free is free no more. Anything or anyone worth having will cost you something. Are you willing to pay with time, love, and patience? If the answer is no, then it is not worth having."

"Being unsure and insecure will lead to inconsistencies. But being confident and secure will lead to becoming consistently sure."

Time of Reflection

When we forgive others, we unlock the doors that have kept us from prospering and being free to love and grow.

Take some time to reflect on a time you had to exercise forgiveness in a difficult situation. Did you forgive, or have yet to forgive? How does forgiveness define who you are today?

Supportive OS Enabling Helpers

"If I fall, will you be there to catch me, or will you be there to drop me? Dropping me leaves me to pick up the pieces. But by catching me, you will be there to help me put the pieces back together again."

"Allowing others and yourself to treat you with past experiences will never allow you to walk in the present long enough to see your future."

"The capability of balancing your life is not an option but it is a necessity to take control of your life."

"Processing thoughts requires acceptance, acknowledgment, and forgiveness of oneself and one another to promote peace of mind without the residue of negative insight."

Life Equations:

Distraction + Division = Disintegration

Determination + Dedication = Direction

"The key to holding your head up and keeping it up is unlocking the door to release everything that is holding it down."

"Stop living your life of yesterday to prove others wrong. Start living your life today to prove yourself right."

"Mistakes made in life are not for you to dwell on, they are made for you to learn from and move on."

"Learning from one's mistakes is never an option to someone who has no desire to change."

"I have felt defeated. I have felt hopeless. But I will never feel like giving up."

Time of Reflection

Do you realize that you were never meant to live your life alone? When you embrace the roles people in your life were designed to fill, you will gain God's perspective on your relationships.

How do you plan to handle your experiences with people, good & bad?

Key Essentials

For

Progression

"Circumstances & Situations of my life seemed cloudy until I changed the way I view my life."

"Be quick for nothing but have self-perseverance in everything. This prevents premature decisions that can promote a lifestyle of regrets."

"Procrastination keeps you where you are, but Determination takes you where you are going."

"Paying attention is free until it cost you everything because you did not."

"Trusting the process means just that. Trust the process and stop trying to manipulate it to work your way. Instead of trusting, you are now in coercion and have become untrustworthy."

"If that was what you wanted, why is that still what you need? It was never about what you needed; it was merely what you thought you wanted."

"Your name, your life, your decisions and your actions should mean more than 'your.' So, mean more, because your name, life, decisions, and actions affect everyone and everything attached to you."

"At my worst I would never want to be negative, at their best they could never want to be positive. Negativity never becomes the person that only wants positive people in their lives."

"If you are not ready to forgive and let it go, then you will never be ready to grow. The decision is not theirs, but yours to be made to move on or to remain stuck where you are."

"You've blamed others long enough. Now it's time for you to take ownership of the part you play and have played to stop the cycle of misery loving company."

"At my worst I would never want to be negative, at their best they could never want to be positive. Negativity never becomes the person that only wants positive people in their lives."

Time of

Reflection

How do you feel when life does not quite go the way you plan or desire? Do you find yourself trying to avoid tough times? Or do you embrace your challenges for self-development?

Spend some time reflecting on your challenges, ow you have grown, or opportunities for growth.

Life Essentials

For

Self-Development

"You've needed help, I've helped you. You've needed love, I've loved you. You've needed forgiveness, I've forgiven you. Only Because I started with me first."

Life Equation:
"Self Help + Self-Love = Self forgiveness. I'm able to help, love and forgive others only because I learned that before I could help, love and forgive others, I must first help, love and forgive myself."

"Have you allowed stairs or chairs in your life?"

__Stairs:__ *levels of life with lessons learned that are worth the elevation causing standing room only.*

__Chairs:__ *levels of life that have allowed no growth, waisted time sitting down while watching life pass you by without realizing even a chair has purpose if it's at the table.*

"Beautiful memories are sorrow for some, but to many, beautiful memories are what keeps them pushing forward every day with a purpose to live."

"Be all in, or all out. Being lukewarm should never be sought out as a popular characteristic."

"Is this your winning season? That was a question. Because if it is, why are you walking in defeat?"

"Bath and Body Works may work for the natural body, but prayer and fasting works for the spiritual body."

"Knowing the difference of inspiration verses desperation will allow you to avoid experiencing desperate situations that will ultimately promote inspiring experiences without regretful memories."

"If you keep your mind, body and soul consumed with unforgiveness, hurt, and drama, you will never have room for forgiveness, healing, and peace."

"I love myself more when I'm not with you. Being with you made me realize I loved myself less. Being without you taught me that self-love is required to first love myself, then others."

Old saying: *"What happens in this house stays in this house."*

New saying: *"I keep thinking about what happened whether in or out of this house, so can we talk about now."*

Time of Reflection

Have you experienced what is called your *winning* season? If so, reflect on how you embraced it, how you felt, and what changes were needed to win? If not, what do you think has held or is holding you back from experiencing your desired, "winning season?"

In past seasons of being victorious, think back to what helped you. Even though this may be a new season with tunnels of hurdles, sometimes what got you through and over then, can get you through and over now by using learned coping skills or effective outcomes that seemed dark and out of reach during an unforeseen time of battle.

Identifying The Core By Destroying The Root Of Deception

"There's a pill under the sun for everything. But if the physical or behavioral concerns are not addressed, you will always have a temporary fix for a lifetime of medical and mental health illnesses."

"Deep dark secrets only need the light of courage to face the truth and finally be set free."

"In some settings a negative is good and a positive is bad. What are some things in your life where the results are opposite of their true meaning, but you continue to ignore the signs needed for change?"

"Positively entertaining bad company can only lead to entertaining negative thoughts."

"While "BRIDGING YOUR LIFE TOGETHER, 2 LIVWELL" you must have the determination to BeWell, by living a lifestyle to StayWell."

"Contentment versus Dissatisfaction. Picking one over the over will leave you with peace or discontent."

"A mind that desires commitment with actions of disengagement can cause a life of avoiding responsibilities that require engagement to commit."

"You chose to entertain until what you were entertaining proved to be negative and was no longer seen in a positive manner. Choose your company wisely."

"Continuing to be someone's meal ticket can only be digested if you allow them to sit at the table and consume your life."

"Mental Illness is only an illness if you never identify it. Once identified, mental illness becomes mental wellness that prevents negative outcomes, occurrences, and disparities."

Time of
Reflection

How is your behavioral health? Your behavioral health is just as important as your overall health. As you explore how to embrace your life's transformation, you must ensure that you are mentally stable.

How would you rate your mental space on a scale of 1-10? Why would you give yourself that rating, and reflect on what you believe gives you mental clarity & stability?

Survival

Strategies

"Being exclusively excluded prepared you to be Inclusively included for your next move for success."

"Being impulsive made you move too quickly. But apprehension causes you to not move quick enough. Being proactive allows you to move in season."

"Your will to survive must outweigh your emotions during your time of despair and desperation to reach your predestined destination of peace from within.'"

"Doing more on purpose does not mean you are accomplished. Accomplishing more to help others means you are doing more with purpose."

"When you think you're at your lowest this is when you're in the right position to help someone else."

"To have peace with power during a pandemic, storm or tragedy can only be experienced through persistent, targeted prayer with unwavering faith."

"Can Purpose implement your elevation? Will Elevation determine your purpose?"

Answer: *"Elevation implements your purpose but, your purpose will determine your eligibility for elevation."*

"Learning self-preservation allows one to live after abandonment, shame, and trauma by removing the guilt of self-abnegation."

"The cost of doing nothing today could deplete your dreams and cost you your tomorrow."

"Your current situation has remained the same. Not because of the lack of help but, because you lack the mindset to implement a plan to change."

Time of

Reflection

What do you think of when you hear the word, "survival?" Did you know that we can use negative tactics and strategies to survive?

Oftentimes we can resort to drugs, alcohol, or food addictions to survive the emotional or mental turmoil we may be experiencing. Reflect on your survival techniques whether good or bad.

Perseverance

Brings

Victory

"You have worked harder at remaining the same while lacking the desire to change by simply refusing to swallow your pride."

Your endurance is dependent upon your mindset, but your mindset is lacking endurance."

"Life has taught you some hard lessons, but your perseverance shows you are living life with lessons learned."

"Survival mode must begin in the mind. If not, being a survivor will merely be a thought that never had the opportunity to survive."

"Awakening with your dreams will never happen until you realize you are sleeping with procrastination."

"Have I, can you, should we? If no, if not, if never, trust and know that premature timing can cost you much more than you can endure."

"Instinct is a God given gift but, it's rarely opened or used to make sound decisions."

"Self-care leads to self-love with opportunities fore renewed strength to continue to be the glue that keeps everything and everyone together."

"You were upset about how they looked at you, talked about you and treated you, it was only a mirror of what you allowed. Now you realize that there is death and life in the power of your words, actions, and deeds."

"Toxic people and situations are different when you recognize that you are the extinguisher."

Time of Reflection

Perseverance.

What does it look like to you?
When was a time in life you had to
persevere, but were not
sure how to?

Have you ever thrown in the towel,
and regretted it?
Let's talk about it.

You Are

An

Overcomer

"Knowing your assignment in life will prevent frustration, disappointment, and stress. Stop trying to fix everything and everyone. Everyone and everything are not your assignment."

"Life is like a deck of cards. Play your hand, sit out a round if you must, but never take yourself out of the game. Winning is learned behavior."

"Have hope. Speak life for endless possibilities."

"The very thing I felt that I could not live without turned out to be the very thing I could have never lived with."

"Staying focused requires clear vision without a cloudy mind."

"I am confused: You ignored and neglected to adhere to the warnings that would have prevented casualties. Instead, you are paying attention to every bump in your marriage, relationships and health crisis with complaints and excuses."

"Having clarity by getting your life in order should cause you to stop, yield and then go while proceeding with caution to prevent crashing into unfamiliar and unforeseen situations."

"Life teaches us lessons, but lessons should never teach your life."

*"By removing the lbs (pounds) that are mentally, physically, and spiritually weighing you down, replace it with the determination to **L**iveWell, **B**eWell & **S**tayWell. Then and only then will you see your WORTH and allow no one or nothing weigh you down ever again."*

"It's My Day 2 LiveWell, Be Well & StayWell."

Time of Reflection

During your self-discovery and reflecting, journal a time when you can say you overcame a battle in your life that makes you proud.

Take some time to celebrate being an overcomer and what your life has been like since you gained victory over what once defeated you.

MAYDAY!

MAYDAY!

MAYDAY!

This is a distress call used to signal a life-threatening emergency. This can be transformed into **MY DAY** when you realize that life is a process.

Just as a butterfly goes through unseen changes in its cocoon, so did you when you were going through and while you are currently going through.

Remember that mental, physical, and spiritual wellness begins and ends by completing the process of transformation.

Stay encouraged, this walk can be challenging, disappointing and even discouraging: But God! Having Him as all you have is all you need. He has never lost a battle.

So I say to you, "Stay on the battlefield and continue to fight this thing we call life without being distressed."

Distressed no more, because your **MAYDAY** has transformed into **MY DAY** with self-perseverance.

Thank you for taking the journey with me.

ABOUT THE AUTHOR

Dr. Monica Johnson

Dr. Monica Johnson, DNP, APRN, AGPCNP-C, PMHNP-BC is a doctoral prepared dual board-certified nurse practitioner of adult gerontology primary care and psychiatric mental health with over 27 years of experience in the healthcare field.

She received several certifications and degrees from 1994-2007. She obtained certified nursing assistant, licensed practical nurse, Associate Degree of Nursing, as well as an

Associates of Arts Degree in Health Care Management from Florida Community College at Jacksonville. In addition, she received her Bachelor of Science in Nursing from Jacksonville University with a specialization in Healthcare Administration.

Dr. Johnson has worked in several specialties as an LPN/RN to include cardiology, med-surge, long-term care, community health, corrections, and nursing education.

She received her Master of Science in Nursing with a specialization in Adult Gerontology Primary Care in January of 2015 from Kaplan University. Over the past 6 years she has provided services in primary care, chiropractic, mental health and substance abuse.

Dr. Johnson completed her Doctor of Nursing Practice program at University of North Florida in August 2018. As a student with UNF, she was the first African American female within their inaugural DNP/PMHNP Dual program to obtain board certification as a Psychiatric Mental Health Nurse Practitioner in June 2018.

While in graduate school, she developed a continued, deepened passion for bridging the gap between Primary Care and Mental Health. Her Community Health background led to a developed interest for patient education regarding the need for appropriate bridge of care to facilitate disease prevention and Mental Health Awareness. Her continued passion as a Doctoral Prepared Dual Certified Nurse Practitioner continues to be helping to serve the community for Behavioral Health with the opportunity to provide Primary Care to promote effective health outcomes.

Dr. Johnson is an awardee of the 2015 Health Resources & Services Administration (HRSA) Nursing Corps Award for working within the underserved and uninsured population. She is also a 2021 contribution team writer for iNSPIRING Magazine.

Dr. Johnson is a member of American Association of Nurse Practitioners, American Psychiatric Nurses Association, Northeast Florida Advanced Practice Registered Nurse Practitioners, and the Florida Association of Nurse Practitioners.

Although she has many accolades, her greatest accomplishments are being married to her best friend (Ervin Johnson) for 23 years and counting, being a mother to her beautiful daughter (Emiyah Johnson), who is a third-

generation nurse and her courageous son
(Ervin Johnson Jr) a soon to be Fireman.

Question: When your life becomes an unforeseen battlefield, what do you do?

Answer: Learn to turn Mayday N2 My Day by doing away with stress that causes an unforeseen battlefield with words of encouragement and affirmations to keep fighting.

Made in the USA
Columbia, SC
06 May 2021

37412450R00082